AMERICA AT WAR

THE MEXICAN-AMERICAN WAR
1846-1848

Simon Rose

www.av2books.com

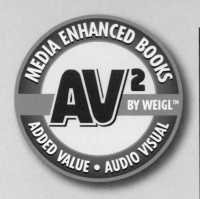

AV² provides enriched content that supplements and complements this book. Weigl's AV² books strive to create inspired learning and engage young minds in a total learning experience.

Your AV² Media Enhanced books come alive with...

Audio
Listen to sections of the book read aloud.

Key Words
Study vocabulary, and complete a matching word activity.

Video
Watch informative video clips.

Quizzes
Test your knowledge.

Embedded Weblinks
Gain additional information for research.

Slide Show
View images and captions, and prepare a presentation.

Try This!
Complete activities and hands-on experiments.

...and much, much more!

Go to **www.av2books.com**, and enter this book's unique code.

BOOK CODE

H439509

AV² by Weigl brings you media enhanced books that support active learning.

Published by AV² by Weigl
350 5th Avenue, 59th Floor
New York, NY 10118

Websites: www.av2books.com   www.weigl.com

Library of Congress Cataloging-in-Publication Data

Rose, Simon, 1961-
 Mexican-American War / Simon Rose.
     pages cm. -- (America at war)
 Includes index.
 ISBN 978-1-4896-1558-9 (hardcover : alk. paper) -- ISBN 978-1-4896-0509-2 (softcover : alk. paper) -- ISBN 978-1-4896-0510-8 (single user ebk.) -- ISBN 978-1-4896-0511-5 (multi user ebk.)
 1. Mexican War, 1846-1848--Juvenile literature. I. Title.
 E404.R67 2014
 973.6'2--dc23
                        2014017384

Printed in the United States of America in North Mankato, Minnesota
1 2 3 4 5 6 7 8 9 0 18 17 16 15 14

062014
WEP310514

Editor: Heather Kissock
Design: Mandy Christiansen

Photograph Credits
We acknowledge Getty Images, Alamy, and Newscom as our primary photo supplier. Page 13 top: Mormon Battalion, © By Intellectual Reserve, Inc

Every reasonable effort has been made to trace ownership and to obtain permission to reprint copyright material. The publishers would be pleased to have any errors or omissions brought to their attention so that they may be corrected in subsequent printings.

CONTENTS

America at War

The United States is a country that was born out of conflict. The American Revolutionary War was a fight for independence from **colonial rule**. From 1775 to 1783, colonists fought British rule for the right to forge their own destiny. Their commitment to the cause established the country as a fierce and loyal **ally**. When called upon, the United States has always fought bravely to protect its values and way of life.

One of the leading characters of the Mexican-American War was General Zachary Taylor. He fought victoriously in many battles and later went on to become president of the United States.

Since its inception, the United States has been involved in a number of wars and conflicts. These include the War of 1812, the American Civil War, the Mexican-American War, and several battles with American Indians. The United States was also involved in the latter stages of World War I and played a major role in World War II. Since 1945 alone, the United States has taken part in conflicts in Korea, Vietnam, Iraq, and Afghanistan.

No matter how a war ends, it usually leads to changes for both sides of the conflict. On the global scale, borders change, new countries are created, people win their freedom, and **dictators** are deposed. Changes also occur on a national level for almost every country involved.

The United States has experienced great change as a result of war. War has shaped the country's political, economic, and social landscape, making it the country it is today.

The Battle of Monterrey took place in the fall of 1846. The three-day battle was the first time U.S. soldiers had fought in an urban setting for a prolonged period.

A War Begins

The United States declared independence from Great Britain in 1776, and the war between the two countries officially ended in 1783. At that time, the Mississippi River formed the western border of the United States, and Americans were already settling in the areas east of the river. In 1803, the **Louisiana Purchase** from France expanded U.S. territory from the Mississippi to the Rocky Mountains. From 1804 to 1806, Meriwether Lewis and William Clark explored the new territory and also traveled to the Pacific coast.

More and more Americans began to settle in the west. Some areas of North America were controlled by other countries, however. Ownership of the Oregon Country in the northwest was disputed between the United States and Great Britain. California and the southwest, including Texas, were part of Mexico. In 1846, the Oregon **Treaty** defined the border between the United States and Canada, and war was avoided. However, in the southwest, disputes between the United States and Mexico, especially over Texas, led to the outbreak of war in 1846.

The Texas Revolution was fought prior to the Mexican-American War. Texas won its independence from Mexico following the Battle of San Jacinto on April 21, 1836.

The Roots of the Mexican-American War

TEXAS ANNEXATION

American settlers moved into Mexican-ruled Texas in the early 19th century. They soon began to call for the area to become part of the United States. In 1836, Texas declared itself to be an independent **republic**. The Mexican government did not recognize Texas as an independent nation, and war broke out. The Texans ultimately won the war. However, Mexico threatened a new war if the republic joined the United States. In February 1845, the U.S. Congress approved the **annexation** of Texas. It became the 28th U.S. state later that year.

MANIFEST DESTINY

In the 1840s, many Americans believed in Manifest Destiny. This was the belief that the United States was destined to expand all the way to the Pacific Ocean. Supporters of Manifest Destiny believed they were on a mission to spread **democracy**, freedom, and progress across the continent. Missionaries traveled west to teach American Indians. Businesses encouraged expansion to take advantage of resources in the West. Ever-growing numbers of settlers meant that new land was always needed. Americans were prepared to use force to take it.

SLAVERY

In the 1840s, the United States was becoming increasingly divided over the issue of slavery. The northern states were growing at a faster rate than the southern states and held more political clout as a result. As the northern states were mostly against slavery, the South felt threatened. Most southern politicians supported a war against Mexico. They hoped that any new states created from the war would support slavery. This would ensure the southern states maintained their influence in the federal government.

CLAIMING CALIFORNIA

California was part of Mexico in the 1840s, but the United States believed that other countries were interested in acquiring the territory. Great Britain controlled other tracts of land along the Pacific coast, including British Columbia and part of Oregon. Some American politicians feared that Great Britain might try to expand southward. They also believed that France had an interest in establishing a presence in California. Going to war over Texas presented the United States with the opportunity to capture California for itself.

A War of Expansion

★ **Bear Flag Revolt 1846**
San Francisco

• **Los Angeles**

The Mexican-American War began as a dispute between the two countries over Texas. However, the fighting went beyond this one region, extending into California, Mexico, and the land that later became the southwestern United States. By the time the war came to an end, both countries had changed considerably in size.

The map to the right demonstrates the scope of the Mexican-American War and where key battles took place.

Pacific Ocean

Legend

★ Major Battle

☐ Mexico

■ United States

☐ Disputed Area

UNITED STATES

Santa Fe

DISPUTED
AREA

Nueces River

Chihuahua

Rio Grande

Buena Vista 1847

Palo Alto 1846

Resaca de la Palma 1846

Monterrey 1846

Gulf of Mexico

MEXICO

Chapultepec 1847

Cerro Gordo 1847

Mexico City

Veracruz 1847

Churubusco 1847

N

0   200 miles

200 Kilometers

The United States Enters the War

Following the annexation of Texas, tensions between the newly formed republic and Mexico simmered. One area of dispute was the border between the two lands. The United States claimed that its border with Mexico was along the Rio Grande. Mexico claimed that the border was the Nueces River, which was further east. In July 1845, President James Polk sent General Zachary Taylor to Corpus Christi, Texas, with an army to help protect the border. A few months later, he sent Congressman John Slidell to Mexico to try to bring a peaceful solution to the border dispute. Slidell was authorized to offer the Mexican government up to $30 million for California and New Mexico, as well as the Rio Grande border.

The Bear Flag Revolt took place from June 14 to July 5, 1846. The flag created for the Republic of California served as the basis for the state flag California uses today.

The Mexican government refused to meet with the congressman, and Slidell returned to the United States, where he reported the results of his mission to President Polk. Realizing that Mexico was unwilling to negotiate, the president ordered General Taylor to move his army into the disputed border region between the Nueces River and the Rio Grande. Taylor then built Fort Texas on the northern bank of the Rio Grande, near to where the present-day city of Brownsville is located.

Mexico did not take these actions lightly. Letters were sent threatening to attack if the U.S. soldiers did not back out of the area. However, General Taylor refused to move his troops. On April 25, 1846, Mexican soldiers attacked a U.S. patrol. Sixteen Americans were either killed or wounded. When news of the attack reached Washington, President Polk asked Congress for a declaration of war. When Congress approved the request on May 13, 1846, the country was officially at war with Mexico.

In June, Americans in Sonoma, California, declared independence from Mexico in the Bear Flag Revolt. They learned that the war with Mexico had already started when the U.S. Navy arrived in California in early July.

James Knox Polk
The 11th U.S. President

James Knox Polk was born in Mecklenburg County, North Carolina, in 1795. He graduated with a law degree from the University of North Carolina in 1818 and moved to Tennessee, where he became a lawyer. Polk entered politics soon after. He served in the Tennessee state legislature and was later elected to the U.S. House of Representatives. Polk became governor of Tennessee in 1839 and was elected president of the United States in 1845.

Polk was determined to expand the territory of the United States. He threatened the British with war in the dispute over Oregon, but later agreed to split the area with Great Britain at the 49th parallel. Today, this is the border between the United States and Canada. Polk's efforts to expand into the southwest contributed to the Mexican-American War.

Polk decided not to run for a second term as president. He died in 1849, only three months after leaving office.

Polk's running mate in the 1844 election was George Dallas, a senator from Pennsylvania. Campaign posters often featured both men.

One of Polk's presidential legacies is the Smithsonian Institution. On August 10, 1846, Polk signed an Act of Congress that allowed for its creation.

Americans Who Served in the War

The people who served in the Mexican-American War came from various cultural and socio-economic backgrounds. Most were soldiers in the U.S. Army. Some, however, were members of individual state forces. These soldiers were called volunteers. Besides these ground soldiers, the U.S. forces also included the Navy and the Marines. Some of the people who served in the war had no military connections. War correspondents, for instance, lived alongside the soldiers and reported information about the war to newspapers back home.

Soldiers

The U.S. Army was not prepared for war in 1846. Officially, the Army had 8,613 **officers** and **regular soldiers**, but the actual number was more likely about 5,500. Very few of these men had any combat experience. Congress authorized the president to recruit 50,000 troops, but most of these men received very little training before leaving for Mexico.

Most enlisted men came from the lower classes. About 40 percent were recent immigrants. Approximately one third of regular soldiers were illiterate. Most army officers were well educated.

While serving in Mexico, soldiers lived in canvas tents, which offered little protection against the elements. Later in the war, they were stationed in buildings, as towns and cities were captured. Basic **rations** for soldiers consisted of beef or pork, beans, bread, peas, and rice. They would also receive some salt, sugar, and coffee if they were available.

Soldiers normally fought in close combat with the enemy. Most of the weapons at the time did not have a long range.

One of the volunteer regiments to fight in the war was the Mormon Battalion. After marching approximately 1,850 miles (2,977 km), from Iowa to California, they were assigned to guard the area around San Diego and Los Angeles.

Volunteers

Volunteers were recruited to boost the strength of the U.S. Army at the beginning of the war. Illinois and Texas provided the most volunteer regiments. The volunteer regiments were known for their camaraderie. In many cases, they were made up of friends and relatives, so they already had well-established relationships and worked well together. Still, they were not considered to be true members of the military. Many of the regular troops felt that the volunteers were poor soldiers. They believed that, because the volunteers had very little training, they lacked the discipline needed to be effective fighters.

THE TEXAS RANGERS

One of the best-known volunteer regiments in the war was the Texas Rangers. The Rangers had gained combat experience fighting American Indians. As a result, they were given key missions during the Mexican-American War, collecting **intelligence** and engaging in **guerrilla warfare**. They often helped army commanders direct the fighting and were involved in some the war's most important battles. Over the course of the war, they gained a fearsome reputation. When they arrived in Mexico City, the locals called the Rangers *los Diablos Tejanos*, or "The Texas Devils."

The Siege of Veracruz lasted from March 9 to 29, 1847. It was the first major amphibious assault by U.S. forces.

Sailors

During the war, the U.S. Navy engaged in campaigns in the Gulf of Mexico and along the Pacific coast. The Navy set up **blockades** on Mexico's east and west coasts. Here, they worked to capture enemy ports and wage attacks on Mexican merchant ships.

On the California coast, sailors not only served on ships but were also involved in the fighting on land. The U.S. Pacific Squadron landed in California at Monterey, San Diego, and San Francisco. Sailors were also involved in the capture of Los Angeles.

The U.S. Home Squadron operated in the Gulf of Mexico. Here, naval forces captured Mexican bases and supply centers both along the coast and inland by traveling up rivers. The Navy also played an essential role in the **Siege** of Veracruz. Sailors helped to land more than 12,000 soldiers on the coast. Some naval gunners fought on land during the siege of the city, using their heavy cannons to help defeat the Mexican defenders.

War Correspondents

The Mexican-American War saw the emergence of a new type of journalist. War correspondents are reporters who travel with armies during wars and report from the scene. There were very few full-time reporters during the war. In many instances, soldiers acted as reporters, sending war reports back to their local newspapers. The professionals that were there worked mainly for newspapers in the southern states. Northern newspapers that sent reporters included the *New York Herald* and the *Jefferson Inquirer*. Other reporters were freelance writers who hoped to sell their war stories to newspapers in the United States.

Jane McManus Storms was the only known female war correspondent and the only reporter stationed behind enemy lines. Her reports appeared in the *New York Sun*.

War correspondents faced the dangers of war alongside the U.S. soldiers. One of the best-known correspondents, George Wilkins Kendall, was shot in the knee during the Battle of Chapultepec in September 1847.

A Soldier's Uniform

CAP

At the beginning of the war, soldiers were often issued **shakos**, but these were gradually replaced with forage caps made of dark blue cloth. These caps had a crown that was soft and wider than the headband. They were equipped with a chinstrap and a leather visor. Forage caps also had a short neck cape to help protect the back of the soldier's neck from sunburn. The cape could be tied at the front and was folded up when not in use.

Soldiers heading to war were equipped with a standard uniform that they wore while on active duty in the field. The uniform worn during the Mexican-American War had not been created for battle in a southern climate. The wool hats and jackets were either too warm in the heat of day or too thin when it became cold at night. Each soldier had a kit that accompanied the uniform. The kit contained all the equipment the soldier was expected to need while away from camp.

JACKET

A soldier's sky-blue jacket was single-breasted and made of wool. The jacket was short but extended to just below the waist. It had nine or ten buttons on the front and one button on each cuff. There were two buttons on either side of the collar. The jacket's cloth shoulder straps were also fastened down with buttons.

TROUSERS

Like the jacket, U.S. Army trousers were also sky-blue and made of wool. They had buttons to accommodate suspenders, and the waistband could be adjusted with a drawstring. The trousers worn by the **infantry** had a small slit at the ankle to allow them to fit over military footwear. A sergeant's trousers had a stripe down the outside seam of each leg.

HAVERSACK

A soldier's haversack was also called a bread bag. This is where the soldier would carry his utensils and rations. The haversack's strap would typically be slung over the soldier's right shoulder so that the bag itself rested on his left hip.

KNAPSACK

A soldier's knapsack carried his blanket, **mess equipment**, toiletries, spare shoes, and clothing. The knapsack had a stiff frame made of white pine. Black canvas was attached to this frame. Flaps that tied in the middle closed the knapsack. Three straps on the top secured the rolled blanket. The soldier's unit number was painted on one of the knapsack's outer flaps.

CANTEEN AND CUP

A soldier's canteen was made of wood and looked like a small barrel. The canteen was usually painted sky-blue and had the letters "U.S." on one end. Most of these canteens were made of white oak, since this type of wood did not affect the flavor of the water inside. The canteen had three metal or leather loops so that a canvas sling could be attached. The canteen was usually carried on the top of the soldier's haversack. A large cup could be used as both a drinking cup and a mess container. The cup was usually attached to the canteen's sling strap.

CARTRIDGE BOX

The cartridge box was made of black leather. It contained a wooden block that held up to 26 cartridges. Beneath the block was a tin tray where the soldier kept extra cartridges, as well as cleaning cloths and spare flints for his weapon. The cartridge box hung on a white leather belt over the soldier's left shoulder, so that the box rested on his right hip. A round brass plate on the shoulder strap kept it positioned in the center of the soldier's chest.

FOOTWEAR

Soldiers in the infantry wore shoes with a high ankle and six eyelets for laces. These shoes were called bootees or ankle boots and had a square toe. The shoes were made of black leather that was smooth on the outside.

Weapons of War

During the Mexican-American War, soldiers had a variety of weapons at their disposal. The U.S. Army used muskets and rifles, revolvers and pistols, bayonets, Bowie knives, and various **artillery** pieces. The Mexican Army had similar weaponry, but it was older and less reliable. This gave the U.S. forces an advantage over the Mexicans and helped lead to many American victories.

MUSKETS AND RIFLES

Most soldiers were armed with muzzle-loading muskets or rifles. The standard issue firearm for American soldiers was the .69-caliber, smoothbore flintlock musket. It had a range of about 100 yards (91.4 meters). Some troops used the Hall breech-loading flintlock rifle or the Model 1841 percussion musket. Many U.S. officers had double-barreled shotguns that they could use during close combat.

BAYONET

Soldiers often attached a bayonet, or blade, to their musket. The bayonet was 16 inches (41 centimeters) long and was attached to the muzzle of the musket. Bayonets were used for charging the enemy or for hand-to-hand combat. When the bayonet was not fastened to the gun, a soldier used it as a general cutting tool.

SWORDS

The Model 1832 Foot Artillery Sword had a 19-inch (48-cm) straight double-edged blade. The sword had a 4-inch (10-cm) cross guard, with a 6-inch (15-cm) brass hilt and was carried in a brass-mounted leather scabbard. The sword was not always used for combat. Soldiers would also use it to cut through shrubs and brush to clear a trail.

REVOLVERS AND PISTOLS

Colt revolvers were favored weapons during the Mexican-American War. U.S. officers and Texas Rangers both carried the five or six-shot Colt revolver. The Colt was accurate within 50 yards (46 m) and was mostly used in close combat. Some older model flintlock pistols were used by regular troops, but were only effective at close range.

FLYING ARTILLERY

Cannons had been used in battles for a long time before the Mexican-American War. However, they were heavy equipment and difficult to move. During the battles in Mexico, U.S. forces used flying artillery. Flying artillery was also known as horse artillery. Cannons were placed on horse carriages and pulled from one location to the other by soldiers riding horses. This allowed for the equipment to be moved quickly and efficiently to where it was needed most.

BOWIE KNIFE

The Bowie knife was designed around 1830. This long-bladed knife varied in size but was usually at least 8 inches (20 cm) long and 1.5 to 2 inches (4 to 5 cm) wide. The knife could slash at the enemy or be used to cut and thrust like a short sword.

Timeline

The War on the Battlefield

August 14 to 18, 1846
American forces enter Sante Fe without a fight after the Mexican Army withdraws. They claim the New Mexico Territory for the United States.

March 1846
General Zachary Taylor leads U.S. troops toward the Rio Grande River. The United States claims the area east of the river as its territory.

May 3 to 9, 1846
Mexican forces attack Fort Texas, but the Americans defeat the Mexican army at the Battles of Palo Alto and Resaca de la Palma. The Mexicans are forced to retreat.

December 29, 1845
Texas officially joins the United States.

The War at Home

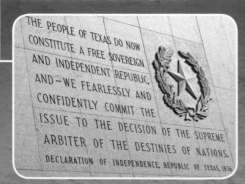

June 16, 1845
Texas decides to join the United States. Mexico refuses to recognize this, and tensions with the United States begin to grow.

March 2, 1836
The Texas Declaration of Independence is signed.

September 21 to 24, 1846
In the Battle of Monterrey, American forces are victorious, but both sides suffer heavy **casualties**.

April 18, 1847
The United States defeats Mexican forces at the Battle of Cerro Gordo. The Americans inflict heavy casualties on the enemy, taking 3,000 prisoners and capturing the Mexican army's supplies.

February 23, 1847
U.S. forces defeat the Mexican Army at the Battle of Buena Vista.

March 9, 1847
U.S. soldiers land at Veracruz, launching the invasion of central Mexico.

September 14, 1847
U.S. forces capture Mexico City, marking the unofficial end of the Mexican-American War.

May 13, 1846
Following the Battles of Palo Alto and Resaca de la Palma, Congress declares war on Mexico.

February 2, 1848
The United States and Mexico sign the Treaty of Guadalupe Hidalgo, officially ending the war.

Key Battles

The Mexican-American War was fought on three fronts. Much of the fighting took place in northern Mexico, but U.S. forces also landed at Veracruz in southern Mexico. From there, American troops fought in several battles as they advanced on Mexico City. Other key battles were fought in California and along the Pacific coast.

The Battle of Palo Alto lasted for only about three hours before the Mexicans withdrew.

Battle of Palo Alto

The Battle of Palo Alto took place on May 8, 1846 and was the first major battle of the Mexican-American War. The battle was fought in the disputed territory along the Texas–Mexico border. It was in response to the actions of the U.S. Army. Under General Taylor, troops had been positioned along the Rio Grande. The army had then built Fort Texas along the river's north bank, across from the Mexican city of Matamoros.

To counter the U.S. threat, Mexican General Mariano Arista moved the Mexican Army of the North to Matamoros. Arista then crossed the Rio Grande west of Matamoros and marched east to lay seige to Fort Texas. Attacking from the east was key to Arista's battle strategy, as it was meant to block the U.S. forces from their supply base at Fort Polk, about 40 miles (64 km) west. The plan was foiled, however, when Taylor received advance notice of it. Taylor quickly assembled most of his troops and left for Fort Polk. Only a small number of soldiers remained to defend Fort Texas.

MAY 1

Upon hearing of General Arista's impending attack, General Taylor gathers his troops and heads to Fort Polk for supplies.

MAY 3

General Arista and his troops cross the Rio Grande on their way to Fort Texas.

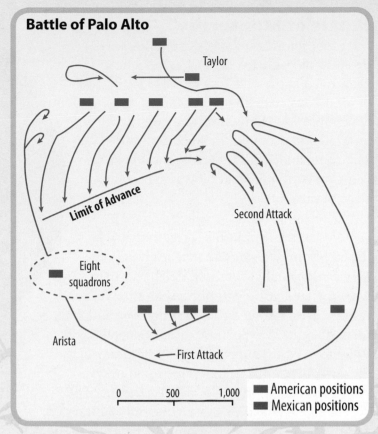

Battle of Palo Alto

Taylor

Limit of Advance

Second Attack

Eight squadrons

Arista

First Attack

0   500   1,000

■ American positions
■ Mexican positions

Upon reaching Fort Polk, Taylor and his troops quickly gathered supplies and ammunition. They then began the return trip to Fort Texas. Taylor had 2,200 men under his command, but on May 8, the Americans encountered Arista's army of 3,400 men blocking the way to the fort.

The Mexican artillery opened fire, but their cannons were heavy, fixed in one place, and used gunpowder that was inferior to that used by the U.S. forces. The Americans responded with artillery fire of their own, with devastating results. This was the first time that the U.S. Army had been able to use its flying artillery. Cannons were moved around the battlefield quickly to where they would be most effective. The American artillery blasted large gaps in the Mexican lines. Arista ordered his **cavalry** and infantry to attack, but they were unsuccessful. During the battle, the Mexican Army suffered between 250 and 400 casualties, compared to only about 50 casualties on the American side. Arista ordered a retreat to a defensive position at Resaca de la Palma, where fighting resumed the next day. The Mexicans suffered another defeat and retreated south toward Monterrey.

MAY 8

Mexican forces block U.S. troops from returning to Fort Texas. The Battle of Palo Alto takes place, and the Mexicans are defeated. They retreat south.

MAY 9

The two armies battle again at Resaca de la Palma. Mexican forces are defeated and must retreat even farther south.

Battle of Monterrey

After his victories at Palo Alto and Resaca de la Palma, General Taylor headed south. He arrived at the outskirts of the city of Monterrey with about 6,600 men on September 19, 1846. Monterrey was heavily fortified and defended by Mexican troops. The commander of these troops was General Pedro de Ampudia, and he was expecting a siege of the city.

Taylor decided to split his forces and attack the city from two sides at once. Although the Mexican positions were well defended, they were too far apart to support each other. As a result, Taylor planned to defeat first one and then the other. On September 20, General William J. Worth approached the city from the west, where his troops came upon heavy fire from Federation Hill and Independence Hill. Worth knew he had to capture the hills if his attack was to progress. His forces stormed Federation Hill and captured Fort Soldado. The next day, Worth's men captured Fort Libertad on Independence Hill. This gave U.S. forces command of the high ground above the city. In the east, Lieutenant Colonel John Garland's troops encountered strong resistance, but managed to enter the city. They captured the Mexican positions at La Teneria, Fort Diablo, and Purisima Bridge, but suffered heavy casualties in street fighting.

Taylor separated his army into three divisions. One of the divisions was commanded by Brigadier General David E. Twiggs, who had already fought in the Battles of Palo Alto and Resaca de Palma.

SEPTEMBER 19

General Taylor arrives in the city of Monterrey with approximately 6,600 men.

SEPTEMBER 20

General Worth approaches the city from the west. Although he experiences heavy fire, his troops are able to secure Forts Soldado and Libertad.

Ampudia withdrew his forces deeper into the city, fortifying the cathedral and the houses around Monterrey's central plaza. On September 23, Taylor ordered his forces to attack on both fronts. Progress was slow, but eventually the Mexican forces abandoned their positions and sought refuge in the city's cathedral.

It was not long before Ampudia surrendered. Although Taylor had won the battle, he agreed to a truce with Ampudia. In exchange for surrendering Monterrey, an eight-week truce was agreed upon, and the Mexican troops were allowed to leave the city with most of their weapons. Although the United States had won the battle, victory had come at a heavy cost, with more than 500 casualties.

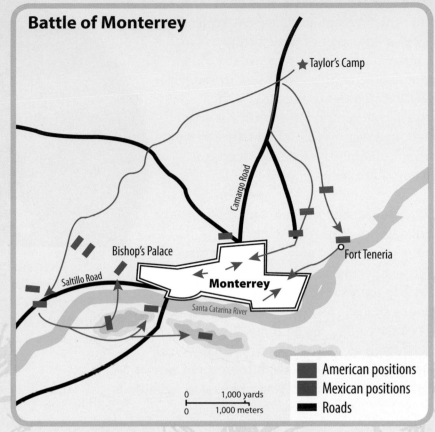

Battle of Monterrey

Taylor's Camp

Camargo Road

Bishop's Palace

Saltillo Road

Fort Teneria

Monterrey

Santa Catarina River

American positions
Mexican positions
Roads

0   1,000 yards
0   1,000 meters

SEPTEMBER 23

General Taylor orders an attack on both the cathedral and the houses around the city's plaza.

SEPTEMBER 25

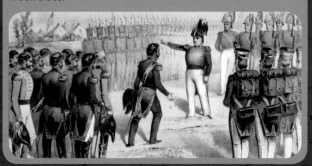

U.S. forces capture the city of Monterrey. The Mexican troops are allowed to leave the city during an eight-week truce.

Battle of Buena Vista

After the Battle of Monterrey in September 1846, a large part of General Taylor's army was reassigned. Many of the most experienced soldiers were sent to another division in order to prepare for the invasion of central Mexico. Taylor was stationed near Saltillo in northern Mexico with 5,000 mostly untested troops to defend his position.

Mexican General Antonio Lopez de Santa Anna decided to strike while the U.S. troops were being moved from one army to the other. Santa Anna planned to defeat Taylor's army and then deal with the U.S. troops heading toward central Mexico. In January 1847, Santa Anna moved north with an army of about 20,000 men. Knowing he was severely outnumbered, Taylor moved to a more defensible position in a mountain pass near Buena Vista.

The First Mississippi Rifles were commanded by Colonel Jefferson Davis, who later served as president of the Confederate States of America. The Confederacy was made up of 11 southern states that separated from the United States over the issue of slavery.

On the journey north, Santa Anna's army was depleted by sickness and desertions. However, he still had approximately 15,000 troops when he arrived at Buena Vista, and on February 22, Santa Anna demanded Taylor's surrender. Taylor refused, and the battle began. On February 23, Santa Anna's forces attacked. By mid-day, they had broken the U.S. line. To save his army from defeat, Taylor was forced to deploy his only **reserves**, the First Mississippi Rifles. The reserves succeeded in holding the line and defeating a Mexican cavalry attack.

JANUARY 27

General Santa Anna begins moving his troops toward Saltillo. He plans to defeat General Taylor's forces before setting up a defense of central Mexico.

FEBRUARY 22

General Santa Anna arrives at Buena Vista and demands General Taylor's surrender. Taylor refuses, and the Battle of Buena Vista begins.

One of the most memorialized casualties of the Battle of Buena Vista is Lieutenant Colonel Henry Clay, the son of a U.S. senator. Clay was wounded on the battlefield. His men tried to take him with them, but he asked them to save themselves instead. He died shortly after.

After suffering heavy casualties, the Mexicans retreated. The Americans counter-attacked, but ran into the formidable Mexican reserves. The U.S. troops were almost decimated before both sides broke off their attacks at nightfall. Taylor expected the fighting to resume the next morning, but Santa Anna withdrew his army.

Both sides claimed victory, but the casualties told another story. Even though there were more than 700 American casualties, Mexican losses totaled at least 1,500. Buena Vista was the last major battle of the war in northern Mexico. It was one of Taylor's greatest victories and is believed to have contributed to his victory in the U.S. presidential election of 1848.

FEBRUARY 23

General Santa Anna's forces attack and break through the U.S. line by noon. The 1st Mississippi Rifles are able to fight back and gain back the U.S. line.

FEBRUARY 24

General Santa Anna withdraws his troops from Buena Vista and heads to central Mexico to fend off the planned U.S. invasion.

Heroic Americans

The men who served in the Mexican-American War came from a range of backgrounds. They shared a common desire to fight for their country. While many performed heroic acts, as the war progressed, some names became better known than others. Some soldiers were hailed for their bravery and strong leadership. Others were celebrated because they performed feats unlike anyone else.

ZACHARY TAYLOR (1784–1850)

Zachary Taylor was one of the leading U.S. commanders in the Mexican-American War. He later became the 12th president of the United States.

Taylor was born near Gordonsville, Virginia, in 1784, but his family soon moved to Kentucky, where Taylor spent his childhood. He became an officer in the U.S. Army in 1808 and fought in the War of 1812. He climbed the ranks and served in the Black Hawk War and the Second Seminole War, eventually reaching the rank of brigadier general.

His exploits during the Mexican-American War made him a national hero. However, his presidency was dominated by tensions between the northern and southern states over the issue of slavery. Taylor was president of the United States for only 16 months. He died suddenly from **cholera** in July 1850 at the age of 65. He was buried in Louisville, Kentucky.

WINFIELD SCOTT
(1786-1866)

Winfield Scott was a U.S. Army general and the foremost military figure in the United States in the years between the American Revolutionary War and the Civil War. He served in the military for 47 years and ran for president in 1852.

Scott was born in Petersburg, Virginia, in 1786. He joined the army as a captain in 1808 and served in the War of 1812. By the time the war ended, Scott had attained the rank of major general. He served as a commander in the Black Hawk War and the Second Seminole War.

During the Mexican-American War, Scott led the invasion of Veracruz in March 1847 and won several key battles, including the Battles of Cerro Gordo, Molino del Rey, and Chapultepec. It was Scott's forces that captured Mexico City in September 1847. Scott was still commander in chief of the U.S. Army when the Civil War began in April 1861, but he retired in November of that year. He died in New York in 1866 at the age of 79.

STEPHEN WATTS KEARNY
(1794-1848)

Stephen Watts Kearny played a key role in the conquest of New Mexico and California during the Mexican-American War.

Kearny was born in Newark, New Jersey, in 1794. He attended Columbia College and joined the Army in 1812. Kearny fought in the War of 1812 and then served on the western frontier.

At the beginning of the Mexican-American War, Kearny led an army to capture New Mexico. He later moved on to California, where he helped capture Los Angeles in January 1847. Kearny was then sent to Mexico, where he served in Veracruz and Mexico City. He became sick with yellow fever and had to return to the United States. Kearny died in St. Louis in 1848 at the age of 54.

The Home Front

The Mexican-American War took place far away from the majority of U.S. citizens, who lived farther east at the time. However, the war did have an effect back home. Local communities who sent large numbers of volunteers to fight were deeply affected by the war. The fighting ignited fierce political debates between those who supported the war and those who opposed it. For the first time, the media played a role during wartime, and new methods of communication allowed people to keep up to date with what was happening in Mexico. The war also led to an upsurge in patriotism, or national pride, and more Americans were attracted to the idea of Manifest Destiny.

The Political Divide

There were opposing political views in the United States during the 1840s. Politicians against the war pointed out that Mexican government had said that it would go to war if the United States annexed Texas. These politicians thought that the United States had deliberately provoked the war so that it could capture territory from Mexico. Opponents of the war also believed that, in attacking Mexico, the United States was no better than European countries and their colonization of new lands. The United States had fought to free itself from Great Britain and establish a democratic republic. Politicians who opposed the war with Mexico did not believe that the United States should expand its territory at the expense of its neighbor.

Most Americans welcomed the fact that the country could gain new land for settlers. However, those who opposed slavery were suspicious of leaders in the southern states. It was felt that the war would be used as an excuse to extend slavery into the newly conquered territory. Former president John Quincy Adams and future president Abraham Lincoln both opposed the war with Mexico on these grounds.

Slaves were rarely paid for their work. Their owners were able to increase their profits from sales of tobacco and cotton as a result.

From *The Bivouac of the Dead*
By Theodore O'Hara

The muffled drum's sad roll has beat
  The soldier's last tattoo;
No more on life's parade shall meet
  That brave and fallen few.
On Fame's eternal camping-ground
  Their silent tents are spread,
And Glory guards, with solemn round,
  The bivouac of the dead.

During the war, many writers and artists subscribed to a movement called romantic nationalism, which promoted patriotism and love of country as an ideal. One of the best-known poems of the era was *Bivouac of the Dead* by Theodore O'Hara. The poem pays tribute to the men who died fighting for their country.

Patriotism

Even though there was opposition to the war with Mexico, the success of the war had a major impact on the general public. As U.S. forces claimed more battle victories and moved farther into Mexican lands, a feeling of patriotism rose among U.S. citizens. People began to identify themselves with the United States as a whole rather than just their individual states. U.S. successes in battle were sometimes celebrated with fireworks and processions in towns and cities back home.

Victory in the war also encouraged the concept of Manifest Destiny. More people began to believe that the United States was destined to rule the continent. In fact, many Americans felt that their country deserved the land in the west more than the American Indians and Mexicans who already lived there. Some people also believed that Americans had a divine mission to bring the benefits of democracy and civilization to those they considered inferior. In 1847, there were even calls for the United States to take over all of Mexico. The idea never gained popular support and was soon abandoned.

The Role of the Media

The media played a far greater role in shaping public opinion during the Mexican-American War than in any previous conflict. Newspapers had steadily grown in popularity in the decades prior to the war, and the newspaper owners were very aware of the public appetite for exciting news. The press used steamships, railroads, the **Pony Express**, and the newly invented telegraph to get the latest news from Mexico. Newspaper reports often reached the eastern United States faster than reports that were sent by mail or by the military

While war correspondents sent reports from the field, other writers contributed letters and articles presenting their views on the war. In 1846, respected American author, Walt Whitman, wrote an article in the *Brooklyn Eagle* supporting the war with Mexico.

Newspapers had a strong presence on the front lines. Besides receiving reports from freelance correspondents, some newspapers also established branches in occupied Mexican cities during the war. The journalists at these branches provided news to the U.S. soldiers as well as to people back home. Articles celebrated U.S. victories and shared the contributions of U.S. soldiers. The reports served to bond the country's citizens and increase support for the war.

In 1846, five New York newspapers banded together to set up a system that would allow them to get news from the war quickly. As a result of this cooperation, articles from war correspondents were sent via horse and rider to the nearest telegraph station, where they were then transmitted to New York.

Today, the Springfield Armory is a national historic site. People can visit it to see how U.S. weapons evolved over time.

Community Involvement

The U.S. Army recruited volunteer soldiers from the various states when the war began. Although officially under federal control, volunteers maintained strong ties to their home states and to their local communities. As many volunteer units were made up of soldiers from specific communities, the people in those communities were invested in the war effort. There was a sense of a common mission among community members, and individuals did what they could to support the families who had men fighting in the war. In the years after the war, many communities constructed memorials to those who did not return home. These memorials drew the communities even closer together.

Even though the war brought losses, some communities also benefited from the war. Soldiers in the field were in constant need of supplies. This created new employment opportunities in some states. The Ames Manufacturing Company, in Chicopee, Massachusetts, made swords and armaments for the war. The Springfield Armory, also in Massachusetts, was the country's main center for firearms production. There was another large armory in Harpers Ferry, West Virginia, that produced weapons for the war. All of these companies relied on local workers and supplies. The money spent on wages and purchases contributed to the economy of the communities involved.

The War Comes to an End

On March 9, 1847, General Winfield Scott, accompanied by 10,000 American troops, landed near the port city of Veracruz, on the Gulf Coast of Mexico. Approximately 3,000 Mexican soldiers were in place to defend the city. However, as the Americans landed, the Mexicans did not come forward to fight, instead remaining in the four forts guarding the city. As a result, U.S. forces were able to lay siege to Veracruz at full power. Scott ordered his troops to surround the city and began bombarding the walls with **mortars** and huge guns, with support from naval forces offshore. On March 28, the city surrendered, and Scott made plans to march inland toward Mexico City.

Fort San Juan de Ulua guarded the harbor at Veracruz. At the time of the siege, the fort had 128 cannons in its arsenal.

Scott's troops pummeled Veracruz with mortar fire for three days. It is estimated that U.S. forces sent 180 shells per hour into the city.

The San Mateo convent played a key role in the Battle of Churubusco. Most of the Mexican troops fought from within its walls, only leaving when they surrendered to U.S. forces.

General Santa Anna was waiting for Scott's army at Cerro Gordo, but was once again defeated. The Mexican Army was forced to retreat to Mexico City. Scott moved on to capture Puebla, the country's second largest city, before beginning his assault on the capital. Leaving a small garrison in Puebla, the U.S. forces advanced toward Mexico City on August 7. The Mexican capital was well defended, and there were a number of battles as the Americans worked their way toward the city. On August 20, the U.S. Army defeated Mexican forces at the Battles of Contreras and Churubusco. The Americans suffered their highest number of casualties since arriving in Mexico, but Mexican losses were much heavier. Scott offered the Mexicans an **armistice**, but the desired results were not achieved. Although there were some negotiations, the Mexicans actually took the opportunity to rebuild their defenses. The armistice broke down after two weeks, and fighting resumed.

Scott launched an attack on Mexican positions at Molino del Rey on September 8. Once these were captured, he attacked the Chapultepec Castle, on the outskirts of the capital city. When the fortress fell to U.S. forces, the Mexican Army retreated. Its government had no choice but to surrender on September 14. Although Santa Anna took some troops to attack the U.S. forces at Puebla, he was forced to give up command of the army in October. The war was over.

The Mexican-American War had profound effects on the history of the United States. The country emerged as a military power following the U.S. victory. Its acquisition of new lands led to more settlements and the creation of new states. However, some of the issues raised at the beginning of the war continued to cast a shadow over the country. Tensions over slavery would eventually lead the United States into another war.

The Treaty of Guadalupe Hidalgo

In February 1848, the Mexican-American War came to its official end with the signing of the Treaty of Guadalupe Hidalgo. The terms of the treaty emphasized Mexico's defeat. The country was required to cede 525,000 square miles (1.36 million square kilometers) of land, including what is present-day California, Arizona, New Mexico, Texas, western Colorado, Nevada, and Utah, to the United States. The treaty also confirmed the Rio Grande as the border between Mexico and Texas. In return, the Mexican government received $15 million. This is much less than it had been offered before the war began. As well, $3 million in debts owed to the United States and its citizens were settled. The treaty stated that any future territorial disputes between Mexico and the United States would be settled by **arbitration** rather than war.

A copy of the Treaty of Guadalupe Hidalgo is kept at the National Archives in Washington, DC.

The California Gold Rush

Gold was discovered in California in early 1848. The news traveled quickly, and people from all over the world flocked to California to seek their fortune. Many of the early arrivals were lucky and became wealthy, finding nuggets of gold in the local streams. However, this was not the case for most people. The people most likely to strike it rich were those who set up businesses to support the growing population. The U.S. government took note of the growth happening in California. To ensure that the country benefitted from this prosperity, the government made California the 31st U.S. state in 1850.

Western Migration

The expansion of the United States into new territories caused a massive migration of Americans across the continent. Tens of thousands of settlers moved into the new lands in the West. This led to the creation of new states and the building of transcontinental railroads. However, the influx of settlers also took a toll on the people already living in the area. Thousands died on both sides, as U.S. settlers and the U.S. Army came into conflict with the American Indians who had lived in the North American West for hundreds of years. The American Indians living in the West were steadily displaced and relocated to reservations, suffering great hardships in the process.

The First Transcontinental Railroad was completed in 1869. It extended from Omaha, Nebraska to Sacramento, California.

PRELUDE TO CIVIL WAR

Slavery had been an issue in the United States prior to the Mexican-American War and continued to be an issue afterward. With the acquisition of new lands came a power struggle between the northern and southern states. Pro-slavery advocates campaigned to have slavery in any new states that were created. Anti-slavery factions opposed this proposal. Debates took place in Congress, finally leading to the Compromise of 1850, which secured California as a free state and allowed other territories to vote on the issue when they applied for statehood. This agreement only clarified the situation in specific parts of the country, however, and not across the country as a whole. The issue of slavery dominated American politics throughout the 1850s and eventually led to the Civil War in 1861.

By The Numbers

Soldiers of War

U.S. forces grew considerably as a result of the war. When war broke out in 1846, there were only between 5,500 and 8,700 soldiers. By the time it ended, more than 116,000 men had served, either as members of the regular army or as volunteers.

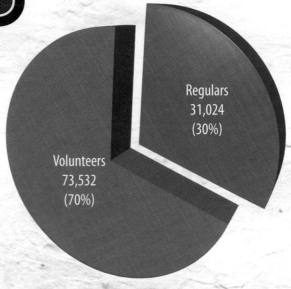

Regulars
31,024
(30%)

Volunteers
73,532
(70%)

Casualty Comparison

Casualties are a reality of war. Both the U.S. and Mexican forces lost soldiers to death and disability. Other soldiers went missing in action. Their bodies were never recovered.

■ United States
■ Mexico

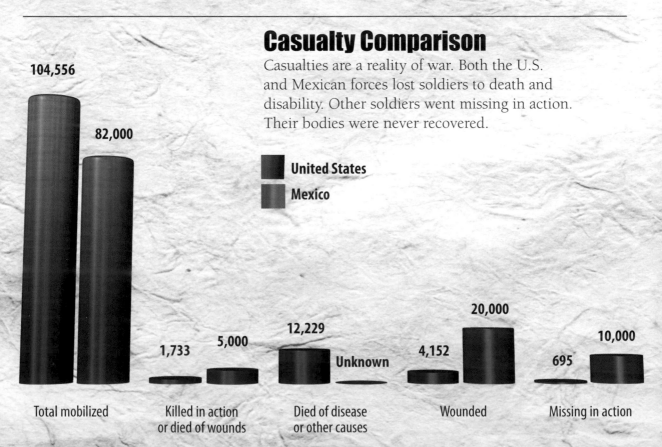

	United States	Mexico
Total mobilized	104,556	82,000
Killed in action or died of wounds	1,733	5,000
Died of disease or other causes	12,229	Unknown
Wounded	4,152	20,000
Missing in action	695	10,000

Volunteer Units by State

Almost every state in the Union sent volunteer units to fight in the Mexican-American War. Some of these men came from state **militia** units. Other men joined newly-created local units and went west to fight.

Number of Regiments, Battalions, and Independent Companies by State					
Alabama	6	Louisiana	11	North Carolina	1
Arkansas	3	Maryland and DC	5	Ohio	8
Florida	2	Massachusetts	1	Pennsylvania	2
Georgia	4	Michigan	2	South Carolina	1
Illinois	10	Mississippi	3	Tennessee	6
Indiana	5	Missouri	8	Texas	20
Iowa	1	New Jersey	1	Virginia	1
Kentucky	6	New York	2		

American Western Migration

Prior to the Mexican-American War, the American West was limited to the frontier. Settlement was in its early stages. The U.S. victory and the discovery of gold in California encouraged people to move west. By 1861, almost half of the U.S. population lived in the west.

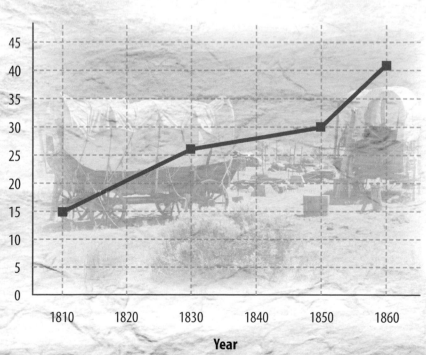

Percentage of Americans Living in the West

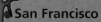

San Francisco

Los Angeles 1846

Casualties of War

During the Mexican-American War, soldiers were seven times more likely to die from disease than they were to be killed or die from wounds received in battle. Still, the fighting took a toll on soldiers from both sides. Some were wounded or killed in major battles. Others became casualties during minor skirmishes.

This chart indicates the number of casualties from each of the war's major battles.

Pacific Ocean

	Conflict	United States Deaths	United States Wounded	Mexican Deaths	Mexican Wounded
1	Fort Brown	2	10	Unknown	Unknown
2	Palo Alto	4	42	100	300
3	Resaca de la Palma	35	98	200	400
4	Monterrey	120	368	700	Unknown
5	Los Angeles	1	142	80	Unknown
6	Pueblo de Taos	6	40	150	Unknown
7	Buena Vista	267	468	1,500	Unknown
8	Sacramento	Unknown	5	600	Unknown
9	Veracruz	12	51	500	Unknown
10	Cerro Gordo	87	353	1,200	Unknown
11	Contreras/Churubusco	164	865	4,000	Unknown
12	Chapultepec	178	673	Unknown	Unknown
13	Siege of Puebla	18	53	Unknown	Unknown
	Totals	1, 167	3,669	12,866	700

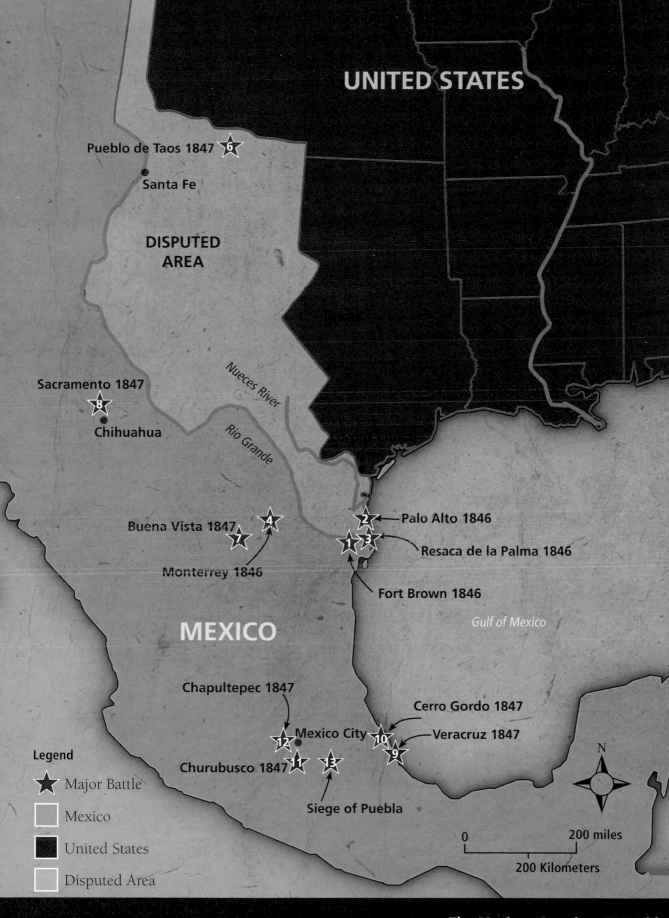

UNITED STATES

Pueblo de Taos 1847 ⭐6

• Santa Fe

DISPUTED
AREA

Nueces River

Sacramento 1847
⭐8
• Chihuahua

Rio Grande

Texas

Buena Vista 1847 ⭐4
⭐7
Monterrey 1846

⭐2 ← Palo Alto 1846
⭐1 ⭐3
Resaca de la Palma 1846

Fort Brown 1846

Gulf of Mexico

MEXICO

Chapultepec 1847

Cerro Gordo 1847

⭐12 Mexico City ⭐10 ← Veracruz 1847
⭐1 ⭐9
Churubusco 1847 ⭐13

Siege of Puebla

N

Legend

⭐ Major Battle

☐ Mexico

■ United States

☐ Disputed Area

0   200 miles

200 Kilometers

How We Remember

More than 13,000 Americans died as a result of the Mexican-American War. Many soldiers also returned home wounded. The war affected people all over the country. People wanted to honor those who had fought, those who had been injured, and those who had died throughout the course of the war.

MEXICO CITY NATIONAL CEMETERY

The Mexico City National Cemetery was created by Congress in 1851 to serve as the final resting place for American soldiers who had died in the area during the war. Today, a monument overlooks 750 American soldiers who are buried there in a common grave. The men were not identified at the time and are known as unknown soldiers. The base of the white stone monument has an inscription written in gold lettering. It reads, "To the honored memory of 750 Americans known but to God whose bones collected by their country's order are here buried."

KENTUCKY MILITARY MONUMENT

Located in Frankfort, Kentucky, the Kentucky Military Monument was built shortly after the Mexican-American War. While it honors all Kentucky veterans, the first soldiers buried on the site were Kentuckians who died during the Battle of Buena Vista in 1847. The Kentucky state legislature commissioned the construction of the Military Monument in 1848. It was completed in 1850. The monument is a square column made from Italian marble. It rises 62 feet (19 m). At the top of the column is a statue of the goddess of war. Arms outstretched, she holds the wreaths of victory.

TENNESSEE MEXICAN WAR MONUMENT

The Tennessee Mexican War Monument was built to honor soldiers from Lawrence County who died during the war. The monument is located in the courthouse square in Lawrenceburg, Tennessee. It commemorates the memory of the Lawrenceburg Blues, local soldiers who died in the war in Mexico, as well as Captain William B. Allen, who was killed during the Battle of Monterrey. The monument was erected in 1849. The base comprises four squares in different sizes supporting the tall **obelisk**. The names of the fallen soldiers, as well as two veterans of the war who died later, are inscribed on one side of the obelisk.

Memorials began to appear across the country in the decades after the war. These were local monuments, developed by individual communities. There are also cemeteries for American servicemen in Mexico. Today, these memorials continue to pay tribute to those who served in the Mexican-American War.

MARYLAND SOLDIERS MONUMENT

The Maryland Soldiers Monument is located in Baltimore, Maryland. The Maryland Association of Veterans of the Mexican War built the monument in 1903. It was originally located elsewhere in Baltimore, but was moved to its current position in 1930. The monument was constructed to honor Lieutenant Colonel William H. Watson and the other Maryland soldiers who died in the war. Watson was killed at the Battle of Monterrey in 1846. A bronze statue of Watson tops the monument. Plaques on the sides of the monument list the names of local men killed in the war.

ARMY OF OCCUPATION MONUMENT

The Army of Occupation Monument is in Old Bayview Cemetery in Corpus Christi, Texas. When General Zachary Taylor was ordered to the Texas border region in April 1845, he set up a base in Corpus Christi. He called his force the Army of Occupation. In 2004, the Descendants of Mexican War Veterans unveiled the Army of Occupation Monument, which was built to honor the 69 men who were known to have died at the base between August 1845 and March 1846. They were buried in the cemetery, but the location of their graves is unknown.

STATE OF PENNSYLVANIA MEXICAN WAR MONUMENT

The State of Pennsylvania Mexican War Monument is located on the capitol grounds in Harrisburg, Pennsylvania. It was built to honor soldiers from Pennsylvania who fought in the war. The decision to construct the monument was made in 1858. It was moved to its current location in 1894. The monument is a column more than 50 feet (15.2 m) in height. At the top of the column is a statue of a guardian angel who has one foot on a cannon. In her left hand is the American flag. A laurel wreath is in her right hand. The names of battles of the Mexican-American War are inscribed on the monument's base.

Test Yourself

MIX 'n MATCH

1. Battle of San Jacinto
2. Bear Flag Revolt
3. Texas Rangers
4. Stephen Watts Kearny
5. Janet McManus Storm
6. Fort Polk
7. Watson Monument
8. Veracruz

a. New Mexico
b. Baltimore
c. Texas Revolution
d. Los Diablos Tejanos
e. Gulf of Mexico
f. War correspondent
g. Supply base
h. California

TRUE OR FALSE

1. General Mariano Arista commanded Mexican forces at the Battle of Monterey.

2. The Oregon Treaty was signed by the United States and Great Britain.

3. James Knox Polk served two terms as president of the United States.

4. Most southern politicians supported a war with Mexico.

5. Most soldiers in the Mexican-American War died in battle.

6. The Treaty of Resaca de la Palma officially ended the war.

7. The Battle of Cerro Gordo was the last battle of the war.

8. Part of the U.S. Army was known as the flying artillery.

MULTIPLE CHOICE

1. When did the U.S. enter the Mexican-American War?
   a. June 16, 1845
   b. April 25, 1846
   c. May 13, 1846
   d. September 14, 1847

2. Which American commander in the war later became president of the United States?
   a. Stephen Watts Kearny
   b. Zachary Taylor
   c. Winfield Scott
   d. Robert F. Stockton

3. The Louisiana Purchase took place between the United States and which country?
   a. France
   b. Spain
   c. Mexico
   d. Great Britain

4. Who was president of Mexico during the war?
   a. Mariano Arista
   b. Pedro de Ampudia
   c. Antonio Lopez de Santa Anna
   d. Juan Morales

5. What was the first battle of the war?
   a. Battle of Cerro Gordo
   b. Battle of Monterrey
   c. Battle of Buena Vista
   d. Battle of Palo Alto

6. How much did the U.S. pay Mexico for its territory when the war ended?
   a. $10 million
   b. $15 million
   c. $20 million
   d. $25 million

7. Where did U.S. forces land during the invasion of central Mexico?
   a. Veracruz
   b. Chapultepec
   c. Cerro Gordo
   d. Molino del Rey

Answers:
Mix and Match
1. c 2. h 3. d 4. a 5. f 6. g 7. b 8. e

True or False
1. False 2. True 3. False 4. True 5. False 6. False 7. False 8. True

Multiple choice:
1. c 2. b 3. a 4. c 5. d 6. b 7. a

Key Words

ally: a country, group, or person in an alliance with another

annexation: to incorporate territory into an existing political unit

arbitration: a process of settling a disagreement through the use of a third party

armistice: a temporary truce agreed to by both sides in a battle

artillery: large caliber weapons, such as cannons and howitzers

blockades: the isolation of areas, usually ports, by ships to prevent entry and exit

casualties: people who have been lost after being killed, wounded, taken prisoner, or gone missing in action

cavalry: a section of an army that fights on horseback

cholera: an acute infectious disease of the small intestine

colonial rule: areas that are under the control of another country

democracy: a form of government in which the supreme power is vested in the people and exercised directly by them or their elected representatives

dictators: people who rule absolutely and oppressively

guerilla warfare: battles featuring irregular warfare, usually involving a member of an independent unit carrying out sabotage against the enemy

infantry: an army consisting of soldiers who fight on foot

intelligence: military information about enemies and spies

Louisiana Purchase: land in the western United States that was purchased from France in 1803

mess equipment: dinnerware and utensils that soldiers use in the field

militia: a fighting force made up of non-professional soldiers

mortars: short-barreled cannons

obelisk: a tall, four-sided shaft of stone that has a pointed pyramid on the top

officers: people holding positions of authority in the military

Pony Express: a system of carrying mail by relay using men on horseback

rations: food issued to members of a group

regular soldiers: people who are professional members of the armed forces

reserves: members of a country's armed forces who are not on active duty but are subect to call in an emergency

republic: a state headed by a president rather than a monarch

shakos: stiff military hats that have high crowns and plumes

siege: when an army surrounds a city, town, or fortress in an attempt to capture it

treaty: a document between two or more countries to agree to cooperate on certain matters. A treaty is also signed to agree on peace terms after a war is over.

Index

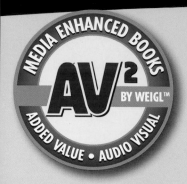

Log on to www.av2books.com

AV² by Weigl brings you media enhanced books that support active learning. Go to www.av2books.com, and enter the special code found on page 2 of this book. You will gain access to enriched and enhanced content that supplements and complements this book. Content includes video, audio, weblinks, quizzes, a slide show, and activities.

AV² Online Navigation

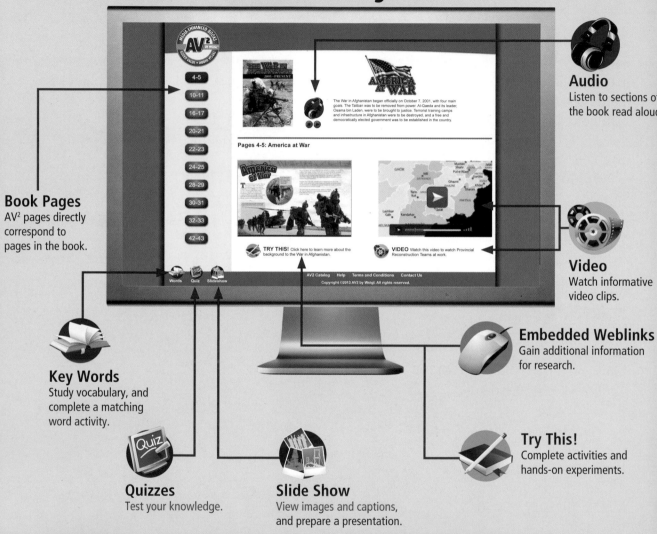

Book Pages
AV² pages directly correspond to pages in the book.

Audio
Listen to sections of the book read aloud.

Video
Watch informative video clips.

Key Words
Study vocabulary, and complete a matching word activity.

Embedded Weblinks
Gain additional information for research.

Quizzes
Test your knowledge.

Slide Show
View images and captions, and prepare a presentation.

Try This!
Complete activities and hands-on experiments.

AV² was built to bridge the gap between print and digital. We encourage you to tell us what you like and what you want to see in the future.

Sign up to be an AV² Ambassador at www.av2books.com/ambassador.

Due to the dynamic nature of the Internet, some of the URLs and activities provided as part of AV² by Weigl may have changed or ceased to exist. AV² by Weigl accepts no responsibility for any such changes. All media enhanced books are regularly monitored to update addresses and sites in a timely manner. Contact AV² by Weigl at 1-866-649-3445 or av2books@weigl.com with any questions, comments, or feedback.